The MAILBOX®
The Education Center®

Organize JANUARY Now!™

grades 2-3

W9-CZL-213

Everything You Need for a Successful January

Monthly Organizing Tools
Manage your time, classroom, and students with monthly organizational tools.

Essential Skills Practice
Practice essential skills this month with engaging activities and reproducibles.

January in the Classroom
Carry your monthly themes into every corner of the classroom.

Ready-to-Go Learning Centers and Skills Practice
Bring January to life right now!

Managing Editors: Cindy K. Daoust, Debra Liverman

Editorial Team: Becky S. Andrews, Kimberley Bruck, Karen P. Shelton, Diane Badden, Thad H. McLaurin, Sharon Murphy, Lauren E. Cox, Peggy Hambright, Sherry McGregor, Amy Payne, Hope Taylor Spencer, Karen A. Brudnak, Hope Rodgers, Dorothy C. McKinney, Cindy Barber, Julie Bulver, Colleen Dabney, Stacie Stone Davis, Ann Fisher, Kelli L. Gowdy, David Green, Terry Healy, Jennifer L. Kohnke, Kathleen Kopp, Kim Minafo, Valerie Wood Smith, Chris Thuman, Laura Wagner, Laine Watts, Joyce Wilson

Production Team: Lisa K. Pitts, Pam Crane, Rebecca Saunders, David G. Bullard, Jennifer Tipton Cappoen, Chris Curry, Sarah Foreman, Theresa Lewis Goode, Clint Moore, Greg D. Rieves, Barry Slate, Donna K. Teal, Zane Williard, Tazmen Carlisle, Cat Collins, Marsha Heim, Amy Kirtley-Hill, Lynette Dickerson, Mark Rainey, Angela Kamstra

www.themailbox.com

Manufactured in the United States
10 9 8 7 6 5 4 3 2

Table of Contents

Monthly Organizing Tools

A collection of reproducible forms, notes, and other just-for-January timesavers and organizational tools.

Essential Skills Practice

Fun, skill-building activities and reproducibles that combine the skills your students must learn with favorite January themes.

January in the Classroom

In a hurry to find a specific type of January activity? It's right here!

Ready-to-Go Learning Centers and Skills Practice

Two preprinted center activities you can tear out and use almost instantly! Plus a collection of additional reproducible skill builders and eight preprinted student activity cards!

Answer Keys

Skills Grid

	New Year	Martin Luther King Jr.	Winter	Polar Animals	Centers	Games	Time Fillers	Writing Ideas & Prompts	Learning Center: Frosty Friends	Learning Center: Cuckoo Cub	Ready-to-Go Skills Practice	Activity Cards
Language Arts												
sequencing events	19, 21	25									88	
literary response		24										
comprehension		29		42								
main idea and supporting details										78, 83		
phonics			35									
prefixes: *mis-* and *pre-*											84	
identifying base words	23											
vocabulary				43		60						91
spelling						60						
synonyms			32									
antonyms				40								
homophones			38	41								
multiple-meaning words											85	
plurals				43, 46								
plurals ending in *-ies*					56							
possessive pronouns						61						
adjectives	20											
subject-verb agreement							67					
capitalization		24										91
quotation marks											87	
writing sentences		25					66					
writing a paragraph		26										
writing dialogue			33									
writing a friendly letter			34									
journal prompts								68				
creative writing								68				
descriptive writing								69				
persuasive writing								69				
narrative writing											88	
support an opinion												91
write a plan												91
setting goals	18											
Math												
number sense							67					
expanded form												93
addition	18			40								
two-digit subtraction without regrouping									72, 77			
two-digit subtraction with regrouping									72, 77			
multiplication facts				41								93
division facts											90	
fact families			33									
identifying fractions	22											
comparing fractions			35									
fractions					57							93
measurement				42								
perimeter		30										
temperature												93
telling time to five minutes											89	
elapsed time			39									
identifying attributes of plane shapes			32									
faces, edges, and corners					56, 58							
flips, slides, and turns			34									
spatial awareness							66					
reading a chart		26										
identifying and graphing ordered pairs											86	
probability					57	61						
problem solving	19	31										
Science & Social Studies												
vocabulary						60						

January

Sunday	Monday	Tuesday	Wednesday	Thursday	Friday	Saturday

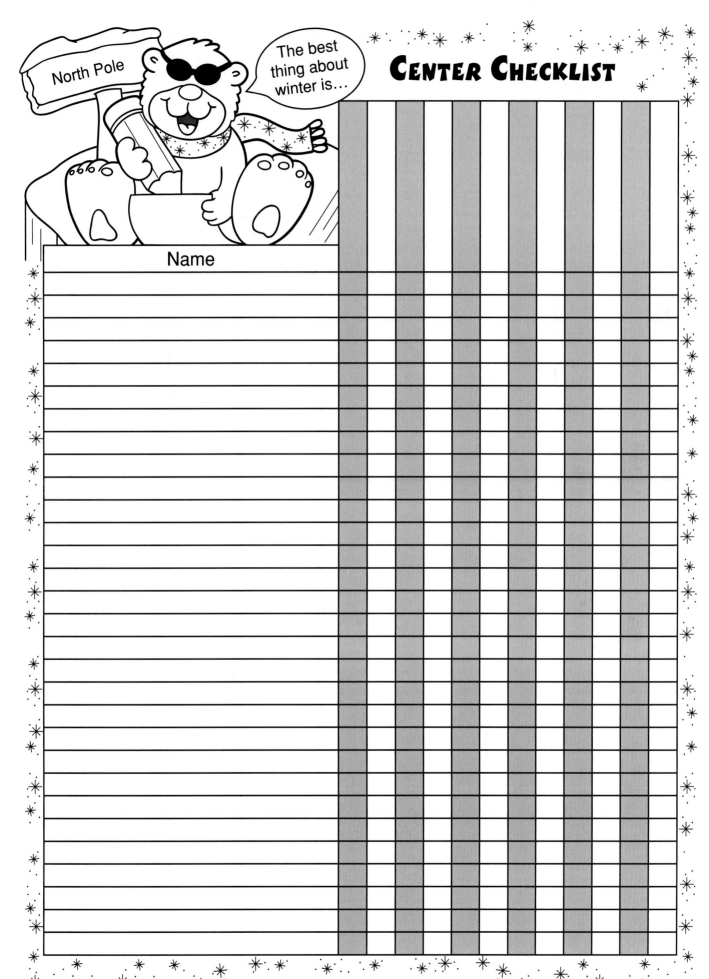

North Pole

The best thing about winter is…

CENTER CHECKLIST

Name							

Class List

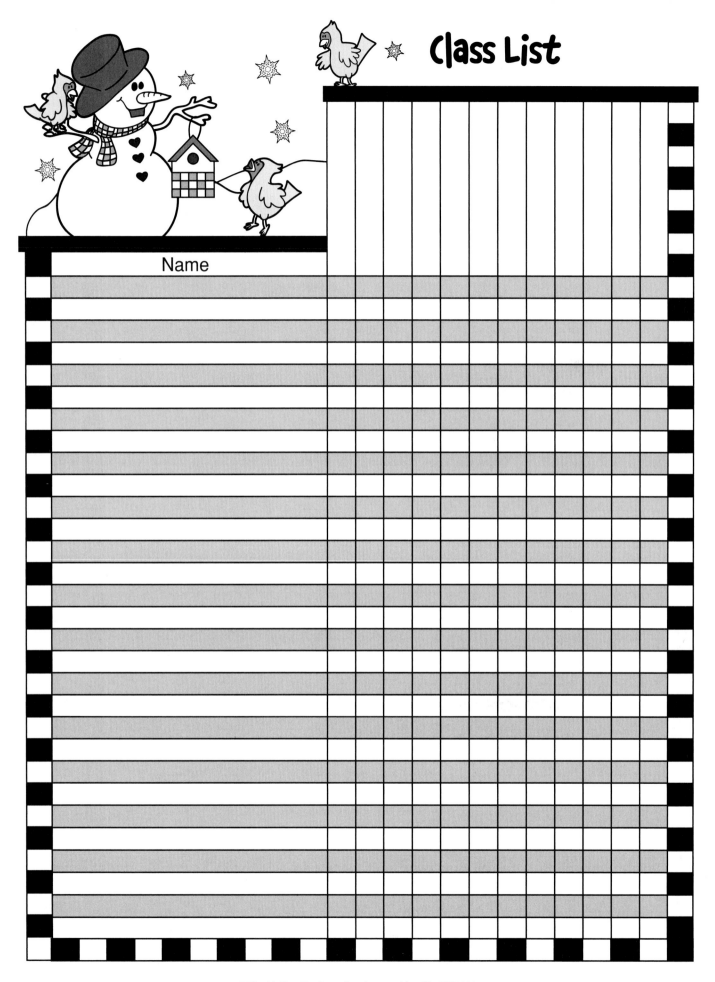

Name

©The Mailbox® • *Organize January Now!*™ • TEC60988

Classroom News

From _____

Date _____

Special Thanks

Please Remember

Superstars

Help Wanted

Check Out What We're Learning

Classroom News

From _____

Date _____

©The Mailbox® • *Organize January Now!*™ • TEC60988

Clip art: Use the artwork on student papers and on correspondence such as announcements, forms, and parent notes.

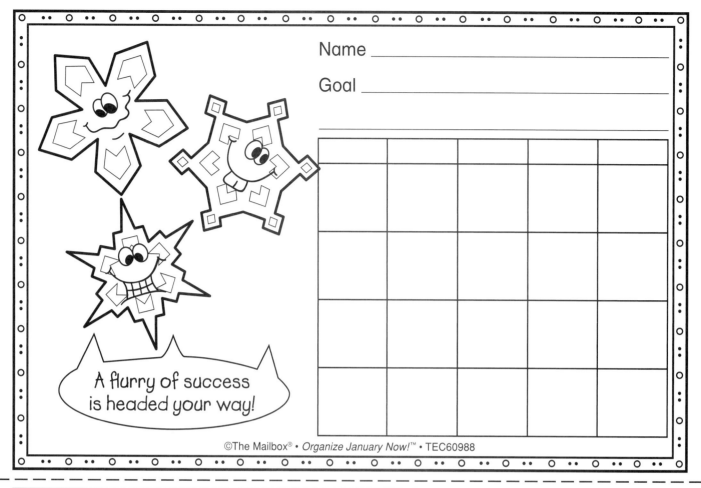

Name _____

Goal _____

_____

Name _____

Goal _____

_____

You are on a roll!

Incentive charts: Have students track their progress as they work toward a variety of goals.

Word Bank

blizzard	nippy
brisk	refill
build	replace
chilly	shift
delicious	snowman
disappear	solution
friends	soothing
frosty	toasty
frozen	weather
marshmallow	wintry

_____'s

Journal

Journal cover: Make this page the front cover of your students' writing journals. Encourage authors to refer to the handy word bank for instant inspiration.

To Do:

_____
_____
_____
_____
_____
_____
_____
_____
_____
_____
_____
_____

Birthdays & Special Dates:

Meetings:

Materials to Collect:

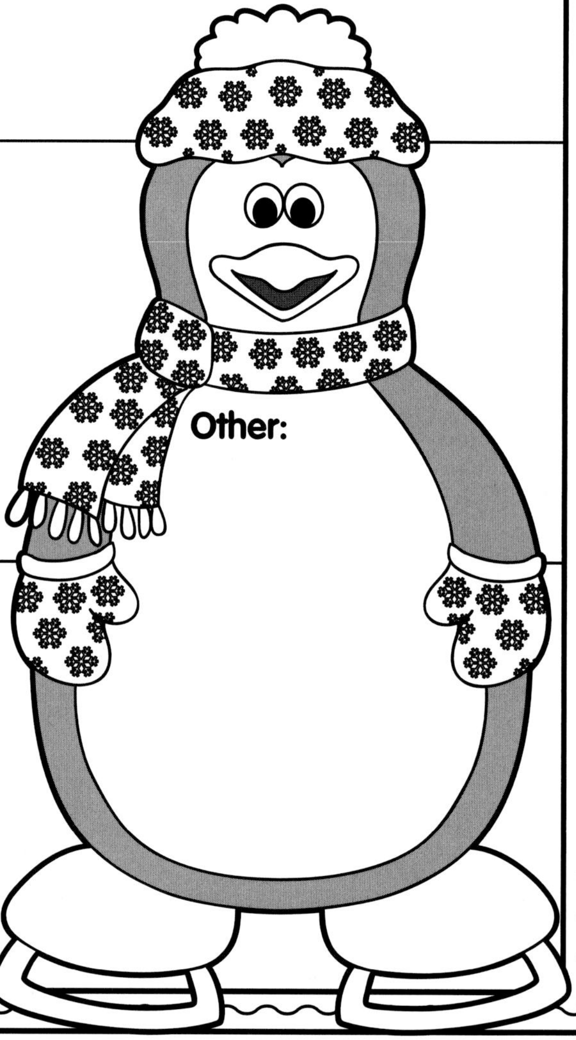

Duties:

Other:

Monthly planning form: Use this handy form to stay on top of January's school-related responsibilities.

Open: Use this page for parent correspondence, and use it with students too. For example, instruct each child to copy a word such as *peace, freedom, respect,* or *fairness* in the banner. Have her write what the word means to her and tell why the word is important each day of every year.

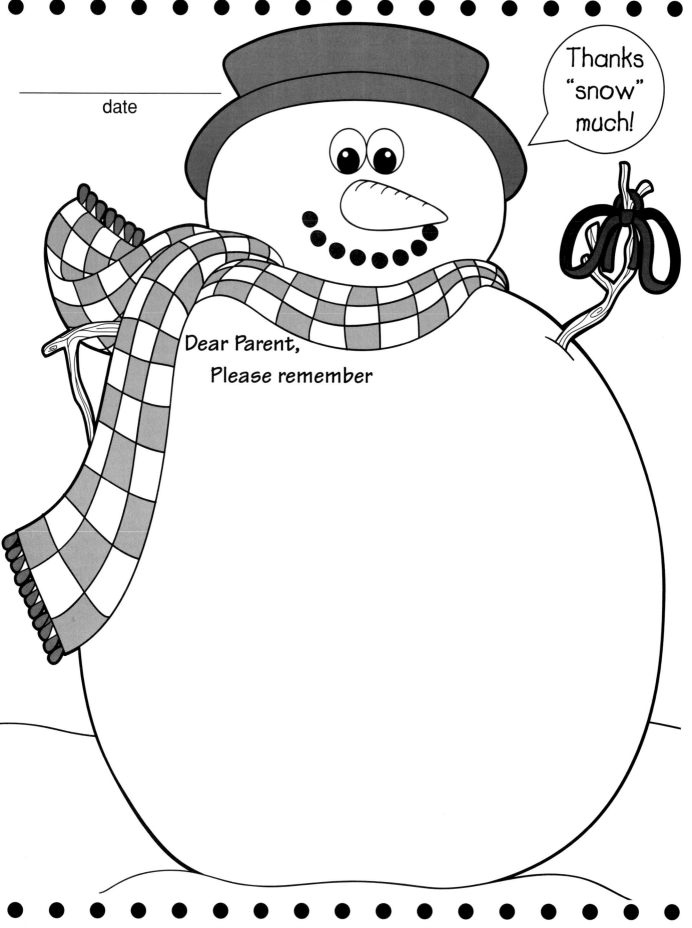

_____
date

Thanks "snow" much!

Dear Parent,
Please remember

Parent reminder note: Use this note to remind parents of supply requests, field trips, and special events such as classroom presentations, school programs, or guest speakers.

School Note

School Note

School notes: Use these notes for parent correspondence such as announcing an upcoming event, requesting supplies or volunteers, and writing messages of praise.

Family Link

Keep an important math skill warm this winter! Have your child cut out the pattern below. Then work together to decorate the winter hat so that a three-part pattern repeats two or three more times. Use whatever supplies you have on hand, such as crayons, markers, buttons, scraps of fabric and fabric trim, stickers, cotton balls, and yarn. Work to make the pattern very colorful and unique!

We hope to see your completed project by _____.

Sincerely,

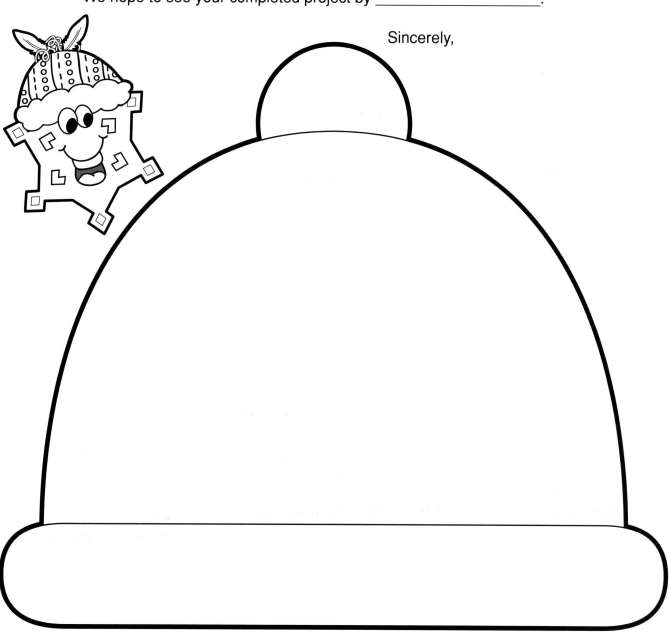

Learning Links: making and extending a pattern

Note to the teacher: Date and sign a copy of the page. Make student copies on white construction paper. When a child returns her project, ask her to share it with the class and identify the pattern she made. Then post her cutout on a display titled "Hats Off to Patterns!"

HOMEWORK FOR THE WEEK

OF _____

Monday

Tuesday

Wednesday

Thursday

Friday

Homework organizer: Program a copy of this form with homework assignments for the week or have each child write his assignments on a blank form.

New Year

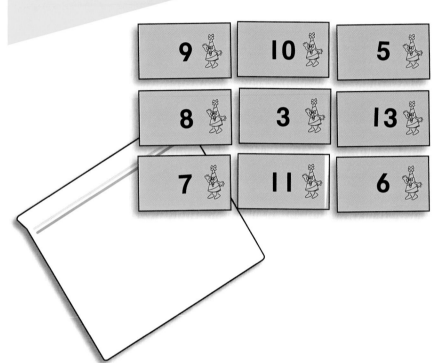

New Year Magic

To prepare this magic-square center, copy the game cards on page 20 onto colorful paper and cut them apart. Put the cards in a resealable bag and place the bag at a center. To complete the center, the student removes the cards from the bag and lays them out, number side up, in a 3 x 3 grid. The student arranges the cards so that the sum of each row equals 24. To increase the difficulty, challenge the student to arrange the cards so that each row and column has a sum of 24.

Setting goals • • • • • • • • • • • • • • • • • •

Ringing Resolutions

Start off the new year with this ambitious activity! Provide each child with several index cards. At the top of each card, the student writes a different academic or school-related goal she wants to attain this year. Below the goal, she lists three things she could do to achieve the goal. Once she has labeled all of her cards in this way, she hole-punches the top left corner of each card and then puts all the cards on a binder ring. When she achieves each goal, she removes the appropriate card from the ring.

I will learn my subtraction facts.
1. I will practice the facts in the car on the way to school.
2. I will write each subtraction fact five times a day.
3. I will keep a list of the facts that are really hard for me to remember.

Ring in the new year with this exciting collection of ideas!

Sequencing events

Looking Back, Looking Forward

Celebrate a new year by providing each student with a copy of page 21. Explain that the Roman god of the New Year, Janus, was believed to have two faces—one looking back to the past and the other into the future. Have each child pretend that he has two faces like Janus. In the left column of the recording sheet, he lists interesting things he did last winter. In the right column, he records several exciting things he hopes to be doing next winter. Then, in the space provided, the student draws a picture of what he might look like with one face looking forward and the other looking back!

● ● ● Looking Back, Looking Forward ● ● ● ●

Name _Alex_

Date _Jan. 5_

Year: _2005_

When I look back, I see...
My brother and me
building an igloo in our
backyard.
Myself helping mom
make snow cream.

Janus

Me

Year: _2007_

When I look forward, I see...
Myself trying out for
the hockey team.
My friends and me
practicing in the ice rink
every day.

Math

Problem solving

Countdown!

Bring in the new year with this brain-stretching activity. On the board, write the date of the new year in the format shown. Then challenge small groups of students to use those digits to write ten different math problems whose answers descend in order from 10 to 1. Once students have mastered this activity, encourage them to count down from 20!

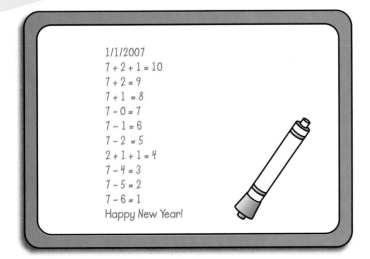

1/1/2007
$7 + 2 + 1 = 10$
$7 + 2 = 9$
$7 + 1 = 8$
$7 - 0 = 7$
$7 - 1 = 6$
$7 - 2 = 5$
$2 + 1 + 1 = 4$
$7 - 4 = 3$
$7 - 5 = 2$
$7 - 6 = 1$
Happy New Year!

Language Arts

Adjectives

Fantastic Fireworks!

To create this festive display, brainstorm as a class a list of adjectives that describe fireworks. Next, have each student write three words from the list on different pieces of colorful paper. Then have the child draw a picture that depicts those three words within a display of fireworks. When he is finished, display his word cards and illustration on a board or wall titled "Fantastic Fireworks!"

Game Cards
Use with "New Year Magic" on page 18.

9 TEC60988	**10** TEC60988	**5** TEC60988
8 TEC60988	**3** TEC60988	**13** TEC60988
7 TEC60988	**11** TEC60988	**6** TEC60988

©The Mailbox® • *Organize January Now!*™ • TEC60988

20 **New Year**

Looking Back, Looking Forward

Name _____

Date _____

Year: _____

When I look back, I see...

_____
_____
_____
_____
_____
_____
_____
_____
_____
_____

Janus

Year: _____

When I look forward, I see...

_____
_____
_____
_____
_____
_____
_____
_____
_____
_____

Me

Note to the teacher: Use with "Looking Back, Looking Forward" on page 19.

It's a Celebration!

Name _____ Date _____

Write the letter of each matching fraction.

_____ 1.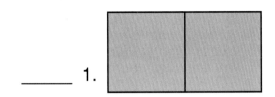

_____ 2.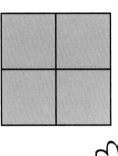

_____ 3.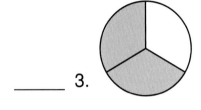

_____ 4.

_____ 5.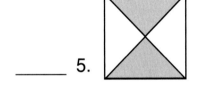

_____ 6.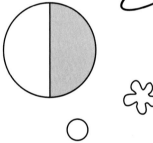

_____ 7.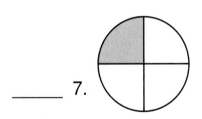

_____ 8.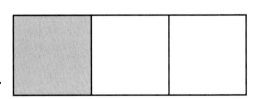

A. $\frac{1}{2}$ B. $\frac{2}{3}$ C. $\frac{4}{4}$ D. $\frac{2}{4}$

E. $\frac{2}{2}$ F. $\frac{1}{4}$ G. $\frac{1}{3}$ H. $\frac{3}{4}$

Party Planning

Name _____ Date _____

Circle the base word in each underlined word.

To-Do List:

1. <u>Untie</u> the balloons.

2. Play the <u>loudest</u> music.

3. Serve the <u>coldest</u> sodas.

4. <u>Unlock</u> the front door.

5. Make a <u>larger</u> cake.

6. <u>Unfold</u> the chairs.

7. Do not <u>misplace</u> the hats.

8. Buy a <u>longer</u> table.

9. Start the party <u>sooner</u>.

10. Do not let my brother <u>misbehave</u>.

Martin Luther King Jr.

• • • • • • • • • • • • • • • • • *Literary response*

Describing Dr. King

Introduce Dr. King to your students by reading aloud a book that mentions King's role in the Montgomery bus boycott, such as *A Picture Book of Martin Luther King, Jr.* by David A. Adler or *Meet Martin Luther King Jr.* by Johnny Ray Moore. Read the book a second time, inviting students to list words and phrases that describe Dr. King. Then have each child write one of his words or phrases on a copy of the bus pattern on page 27. He cuts out the pattern and adds it to a display. As students learn more about Dr. King, they add additional buses to the display. Encourage them to use this word bank to write original poems, letters, or other writing pieces about this great man.

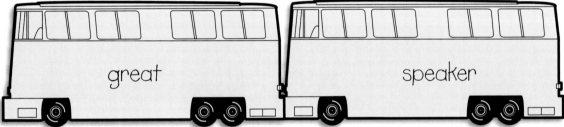

Capitalization • • • • • • • • • • • • • • • • • •

A Capital Idea

For a simple center that builds capitalization skills, make two copies of the cards at the top of page 28. Cut apart the cards from one copy. To make an answer key, cut out the entire set of cards on the second copy, as shown, and circle the letters that need capitalization. Store the cards and key in a zippered bag. To complete the center, each student numbers her paper from 1 to 15. She selects a card and rewrites it next to the corresponding number on her paper, using the correct capitalization. After completing all 15 cards, the student checks her work with the key. Then she selects one card and writes a sentence describing how the item on it relates to Dr. King.

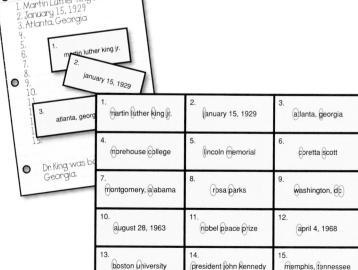

Teach students about Dr. Martin Luther King, Jr. and reinforce skills with these memorable activities.

Writing sentences • • • • • • • • • • • • • • • •

Sentence Sense

Begin this activity by reviewing the four types of sentences: statement, question, exclamation, and command. Then give each student a sentence strip. The student uses one of the four types of sentences to write on his strip a sentence about Dr. King. After he reads his sentence aloud, he calls on a classmate to identify the type of sentence it represents. After that classmate answers, she reads her sentence aloud. When every child has shared her sentence, organize the strips on a wall by sentence type. If desired, have students create additional sentences to add to the display.

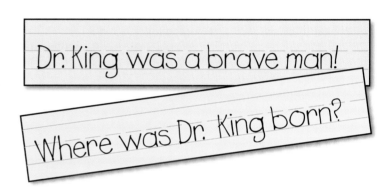

• • • • • • • • • • • • • • • *Sequencing events*

An Extraordinary Life

After reading and discussing information about Dr. King, have students brainstorm the important events in his life (see the list on page 28). As a class, sequence the events (see the key at left). Then give each student or student pair eight copies of the bus pattern on page 27 and one copy of the event cards on page 28. The student first cuts out and tapes together the bus cutouts in a line. After titling the first pattern, she cuts out and glues the events in order on the remaining patterns. Finally, she accordion-folds the bus patterns to make a booklet.

Correct sequence of events:
1. Martin Luther King Jr. is born.
2. Martin Luther King Jr. becomes a minister.
3. Martin Luther King Jr. marries Coretta Scott.
4. Dr. King leads the bus boycott in Montgomery, Alabama.
5. Dr. King gives a speech in Washington, DC. He says, "I have a dream."
6. Dr. King wins the Nobel Peace Prize.
7. Dr. King is shot and killed.

Language Arts

Turn This World Upside Down

A young Martin Luther King once told his mother, "I'm going to turn this world upside down." Discuss with students what he meant and how Dr. King truly did change the world. Then challenge each child to think of a way that he would like to change the world for the better. Have him label a large index card with a short paragraph that describes his idea. To display his paragraph, he colors a small white paper plate or circle to resemble a globe. He tapes one end of a yarn length to the back of the globe and the other end to the back of his paragraph. Then he staples his project on a bulletin board titled "Watch Us Turn This World Upside Down!"

Math

Parading the Weather

Many cities celebrate Martin Luther King Jr. Day with parades. Identify which ones will enjoy the best parade weather by creating the chart shown, which lists cities related to Dr. King's life. Help students locate each city on a map. Then, each day during the third week in January, assist a different student in locating an online weather site and finding each city's high temperature and expected precipitation for the day. The student records the information on the chart. At week's end, students examine the chart to determine which cities had the best and worst weather for their Martin Luther King Jr. Day celebrations.

Find reproducible activities on pages 29–31.

	Jan. 15	Jan. 16	Jan. 17	Jan. 18	Jan. 19
Atlanta, GA	58°F				
Washington, DC	48°F				
Montgomery, AL	55°F				
Boston, MA	15°F				
Memphis, TN	34°F				

Use with "Describing Dr. King" on page 24 and "An Extraordinary Life" on page 25.

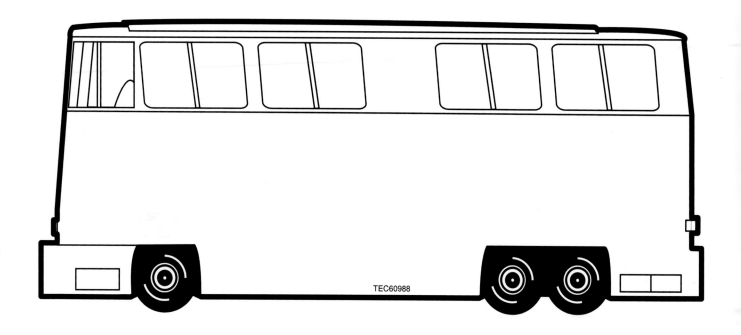

TEC60988

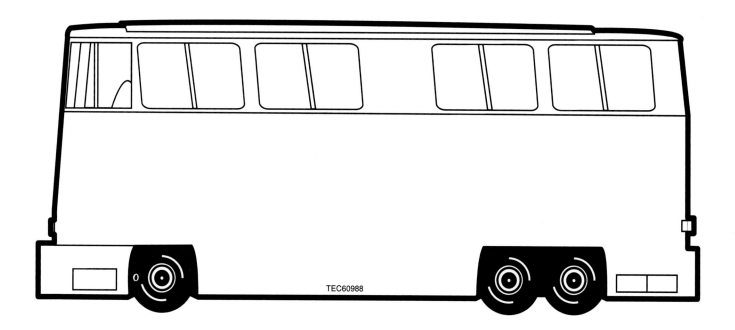

TEC60988

Capitalization Cards

Use with "A Capital Idea" on page 24.

1. martin luther king jr. TEC60988	2. january 15, 1929 TEC60988	3. atlanta, georgia TEC60988
4. morehouse college TEC60988	5. lincoln memorial TEC60988	6. coretta scott TEC60988
7. montgomery, alabama TEC60988	8. rosa parks TEC60988	9. washington, dc TEC60988
10. august 28, 1963 TEC60988	11. nobel peace prize TEC60988	12. april 4, 1968 TEC60988
13. boston university TEC60988	14. president john kennedy TEC60988	15. memphis, tennessee TEC60988

Event Cards

Use with "An Extraordinary Life" on page 25.

Martin Luther King Jr. marries Coretta Scott. TEC60988	Dr. King gives a speech in Washington, DC. He says, "I have a dream." TEC60988	Martin Luther King Jr. is born. TEC60988	Dr. King is shot and killed. TEC60988	Martin Luther King Jr. becomes a minister. TEC60988	Dr. King wins the Nobel Peace Prize. TEC60988	Dr. King leads the bus boycott in Montgomery, Alabama. TEC60988

Martin Luther King Jr. Day

Name _____

Date _____

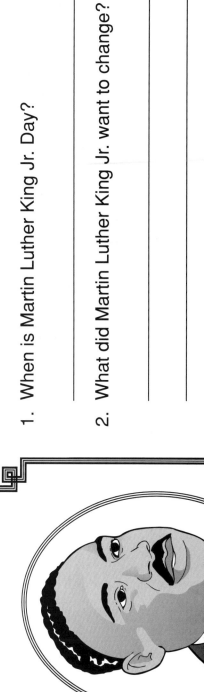

Dr. Martin Luther King Jr. was born on January 15, 1929. We celebrate this day on the third Monday in January.

When he was a child, Martin Luther King Jr. saw that black people were treated differently than white people. They could not go to the same schools. They could not eat at the same restaurants or use the same water fountains. Martin knew that this was wrong. When he grew up he worked in peaceful ways to get laws changed. He led marches. He gave speeches. He sometimes sat in silence. Often he was arrested and put in jail for standing up for his beliefs.

People noticed. Laws were changed to help black people. But some people did not want change. They wanted to fight. One day, a man shot and killed Dr. King. Today we remember Dr. Martin Luther King Jr. We know him as a brave leader. His dream of equality brings hope for all people.

1. When is Martin Luther King Jr. Day?
   _____

2. What did Martin Luther King Jr. want to change?
   _____
   _____

3. Circle three things that Dr. King did to get unfair laws changed.

4. Write two words that describe Martin Luther King Jr.
   _____

5. What do you think the word *equality* means?
   _____
   _____

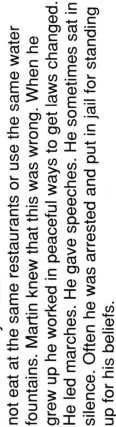

©The Mailbox® • *Organize January Now!*™ • TEC60988 • Key p. 95

Name _____

Date _____

Follow the Parade!

Use a centimeter ruler.
Measure the perimeter of each shape.
Write your answers below.

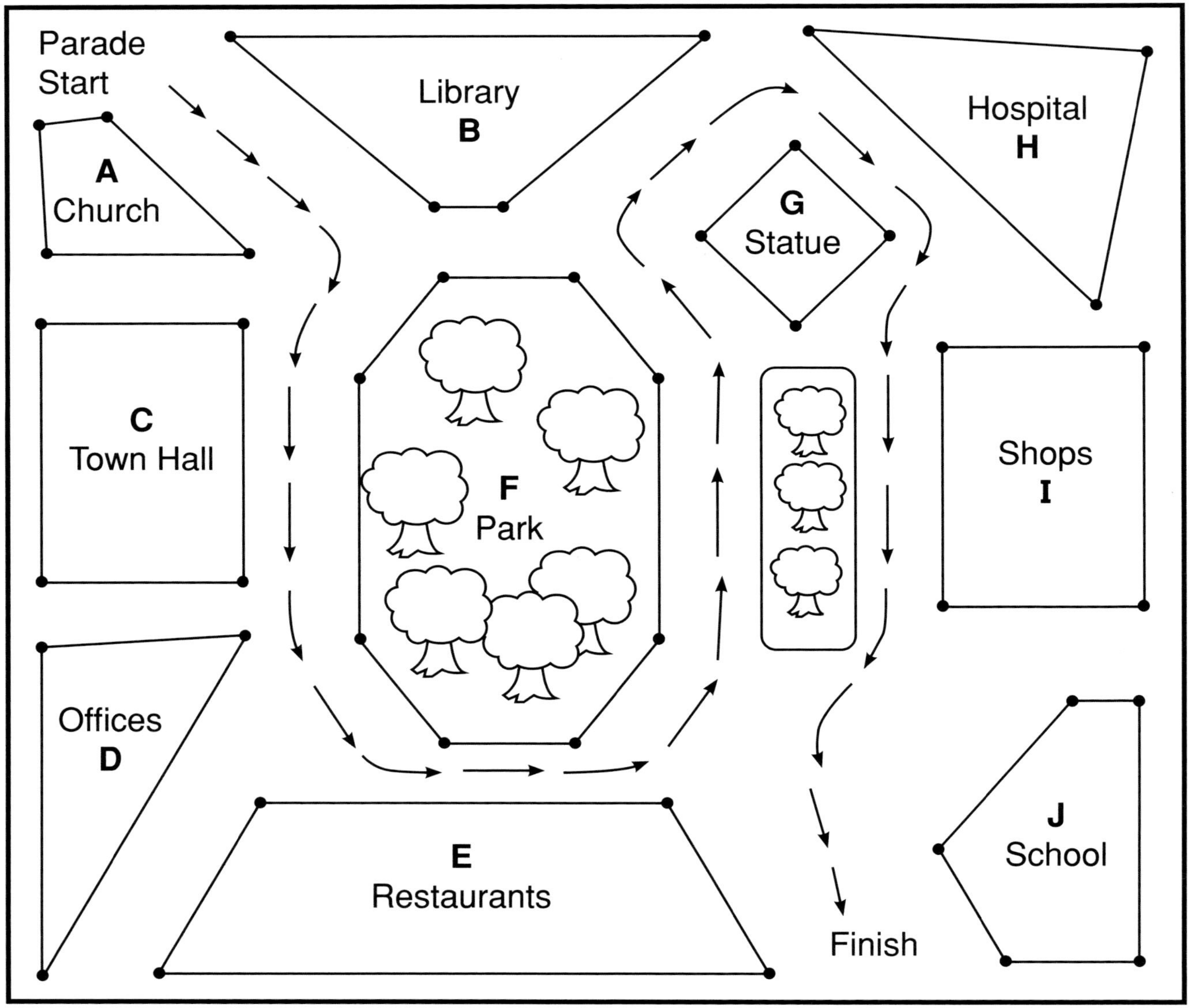

A. _____ cm
B. _____ cm
C. _____ cm
D. _____ cm
E. _____ cm
F. _____ cm
G. _____ cm
H. _____ cm
I. _____ cm
J. _____ cm

Happy Martin
Luther King
Jr. Day!

Parade Start

A Church

C Town Hall

Offices D

Library B

F Park

E Restaurants

G Statue

Hospital H

Shops I

J School

Finish

Perimeter

Celebrating Dr. King

Name_____   Date _____

Sara, Mark, Tyrone, and Kate are planning a party
    for Martin Luther King Jr. Day.
Use the clues to solve each problem.

A. What food will each child bring?
   Clues:
   1. Sara will not bring drinks or chips.
   2. Tyrone will bring cookies.
   3. A boy will bring drinks.
   4. A girl will bring chips.

	Sara	Mark	Tyrone	Kate
Drinks				
Chips				
Hot dogs				
Cookies				

Sara   _____

Mark   _____

Tyrone _____

Kate   _____

B. Where will each child sit?
   Clues:
   1. Kate will sit between Sara and Mark.
   2. Tyrone will sit in the last chair.
   3. Sara will sit between two people.

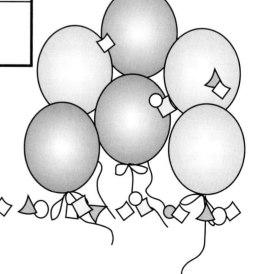

_____ _____ _____ _____

Winter

Math • • • • • • • • • • Identifying attributes of plane shapes

Stocking-Cap Surprises

To prepare this center, cut out different sizes of colorful paper polygons, such as squares, rectangles, circles, and triangles. Also gather several stocking caps. Arrange the caps in a row at a center with writing paper. Under each cap, hide several different cutouts. To use the center, a child lifts any cap, writes the names of the shapes he uncovered, and lists the attributes of each one. When he's finished, he replaces the cap and chooses a different cap to lift. He continues in this manner as long as time allows.

Synonyms • • • • • • • • • • • • • Language Arts

A Flurry of Synonyms

Give each student a 6" x 12" blue construction paper rectangle, a five-inch white construction paper circle, scissors, glue, and a white crayon. The child makes a snowflake by folding and cutting the white circle as shown. She positions the blue paper horizontally and then glues the snowflake on the left side. On the right side of the paper, she uses the white crayon to write a word that describes the snowflake. Under the word, she lists as many synonyms for that adjective as she can. Post the completed projects on a bulletin board titled "A Flurry of Synonyms."

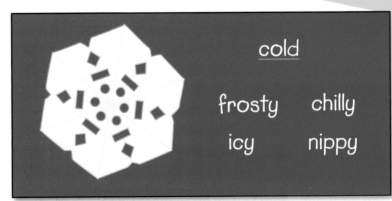

Fold.

Fold.

Fold.

Cut. Unfold.

Brrr! When it's cold outside, warm up students' math and language skills with this inviting collection of activities and reproducibles!

Fact families • • • • • • • • • • • • • • • • • Math

Sweet Fluffs and Puffs

Prepare this center by cutting eight 3" x 5" index cards in half. Program each piece with a different fact shown; then glue a cotton ball on the back of each piece to resemble a marshmallow. To make the center self-checking, use permanent markers to put a different colored dot on the back of each set of four cards. Put the cards in a plastic resealable bag and then place the bag at a center along with four large foam cups. Each visitor to the center sorts the cards by fact family into separate cups and then pours out each set and checks his work.

4 x 3

3 x 4

12 ÷ 4

12 ÷ 3

4 x 3	2 x 8	7 x 1	4 x 6
3 x 4	8 x 2	1 x 7	6 x 4
12 ÷ 4	16 ÷ 2	7 ÷ 1	24 ÷ 4
12 ÷ 3	16 ÷ 8	7 ÷ 7	24 ÷ 6

Language Arts • • • • • • • • • • • • • • Writing dialogue

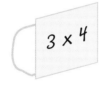

Characters

Events

Ruby Rabbit

Betsy Bear

Two friends work together to shovel the driveway.

Speaking of Winter

To prepare for this partner activity, cut apart the character and event cards on page 36. Put each set of cards in a different brown paper lunch bag and place at a center the bags and writing paper. Invite a student pair to draw from the bags two character cards and one event card. One partner records at the top of a sheet of paper the information from the cards and then returns the cards to the correct bags. Next, the partners brainstorm a conversation that the two characters could have in the given situation. Then they record the conversation on their paper, using correct punctuation and capitalization.

Ruby Rabbit
Betsy Bear
Two friends work together to shovel the driveway.
"Shoveling this driveway is hard work!" Ruby Rabbit said.
"Yes, but it feels good to help our neighbor," Betsy Bear said.
"You're right," said Ruby.
"Let's do a really good job!" said Betsy.
"Then we can have cocoa at my house," said Ruby.

Mitten Movements

Give each student a 9" x 24" construction paper strip, a colorful index card, and a mitten template such as the one shown. Direct the child to use the template and the index card to make a mitten cutout. Have him trace the mitten on the left end of the long paper strip as shown. Next, call out "Flip," "Slide," or "Turn," and guide him to move the cutout as directed and then trace the mitten in its new position. Continue in this manner as time allows.

Cool Cards

Writing these postcards lets students share their thoughts about winter weather in their area. Have each child draw a scene depicting winter weather on one side of a 9" x 12" piece of white construction paper. Next, have her think about what she does on a typical winter day. On the back of the paper, have her write a postcard to a friend about her winter day. When all students have finished, invite each child to share her letter and drawing with the class.

January 7, 2007

Dear Stan,
    It sure was cold today. My family and I went sledding in the park. I was so cold that my fingers hurt. I couldn't wait to get home and drink hot cocoa. Later, we ordered a pizza and watched some movies. It was a great day!

Your friend,
Lynn

Stan Sunshine
1234 Beach Road
Orange, Florida
    10000

Gotta Hand It to You

This center provides hands-on sorting practice! On a piece of construction paper, write in random order the word groups shown. Post the list in a center. Make a template of an oversized glove and place it at the center along with scissors, markers, and a supply of 9" x 12" sheets of construction paper. Direct each child who visits the center to make one glove cutout. Next, the child writes the word *snow* in the center of one side of the cutout and the word *how* in the center of the other side. He decides whether each listed word has the sound he hears in *snow* or the sound he hears in *how*. Then he writes the word on one finger or thumb on the matching side of the glove. He continues until he has written all ten words.

A Fractional Snowball Fight

For this two-player game, have each student pair cut apart one copy of the cards on page 37. In addition, give the pair a set of fraction models for halves, thirds, fourths, and sixths. To play, one player shuffles the cards and distributes all of the cards between the two players. Each player places his stack of cards facedown in front of him. At the same time, each player turns over his top card. They study the cards, using the models as needed, to determine which player's card represents the greater amount. That player takes both cards. If the amounts are equal, each player turns over the next card in the stack and the players compare those cards. The player whose second card has the higher amount takes all four cards. Play continues as time allows. The player with more cards wins.

Find reproducible activities on pages 38–39.

Marvin Moose
TEC60988

Freddy Fox
TEC60988

Rachel Raccoon
TEC60988

Betsy Bear
TEC60988

Sammy Skunk
TEC60988

Ruby Rabbit
TEC60988

One friend calls another to plan a trip to the ice-skating pond.
TEC60988

Two friends meet at a restaurant for hot cocoa and doughnuts.
TEC60988

Two friends build a snowman in the park.
TEC60988

Two friends paint a snow scene in art class.
TEC60988

Two friends work together to shovel the driveway.
TEC60988

Two friends plan a winter party.
TEC60988

$\frac{2}{3}$ TEC60988	$\frac{3}{6}$ TEC60988	$\frac{1}{4}$ TEC60988
$\frac{1}{3}$ TEC60988	$\frac{2}{6}$ TEC60988	$\frac{1}{3}$ TEC60988
$\frac{3}{4}$ TEC60988	$\frac{1}{6}$ TEC60988	$\frac{1}{2}$ TEC60988
$\frac{2}{4}$ TEC60988	$\frac{3}{3}$ TEC60988	$\frac{6}{6}$ TEC60988
$\frac{1}{4}$ TEC60988	$\frac{4}{4}$ TEC60988	$\frac{5}{6}$ TEC60988
$\frac{1}{2}$ TEC60988	$\frac{2}{2}$ TEC60988	$\frac{4}{6}$ TEC60988

Frozen Fun

Name_____ Date _____

Color the skate with the word that best completes each sentence.

1. Today is a _____ day for skating!

   E. great   L. grate

2. The _____ is shining on the smooth ice.

   B. son   M. sun

3. _____ of my friends are going too.

   P. Four   T. For

4. I will meet them in one _____.

   T. hour   E. our

5. We will _____ at the pond.

   A. meat   K. meet

6. I hope we have the _____ pond to ourselves.

   I. whole   D. hole

7. We will stay _____ until dinnertime.

   G. their   U. there

8. I don't want to get too _____.

   S. chili   H. chilly

9. I will wear plenty of warm _____.

   A. clothes   R. close

10. I can't _____ to show off my new skates!

   K. weight   C. wait

Why shouldn't you tell jokes when you're ice-skating?
To solve the riddle, write the colored letters above on the numbered lines below.

Because __ __ __   __ __ __   __ __ __ G __   __ R __   __ __ __ __!
        4 8 1   6 10 1   2 6   8 4   10   9 10 5   7 3

©The Mailbox® • *Organize January Now!*™ • TEC60988 • Key p. 95

Hockey Time

Name _____ Date _____

Read.
Solve.

A. The team began practice at 7:15 A.M. They finished at 8:40 A.M. How long did they practice?

___ hour ___ minutes

B. The team meeting began at 8:50 A.M. It ended at 9:25 A.M. How long was the meeting?

___ minutes

C. Ben began wrapping his hockey stick at 3:20 P.M. He finished at 3:35 P.M. How long did it take him to wrap the stick?

___ minutes

D. The visiting team got on the bus at 4:35 P.M. They got to the arena at 4:55 P.M. How long was their trip?

___ minutes

E. The players began to get dressed at 5:45 P.M. They finished at 6:25 P.M. How long did it take them to get dressed?

___ minutes

F. Fans began to arrive at 5:35 P.M. The last fan came in at 6:50 P.M. How long did it take for all of the fans to arrive?

___ hour ___ minutes

G. The game began at 7:05 P.M. It ended at 9:10 P.M. How long was the game?

___ hours ___ minutes

H. The Zamboni machine began scraping the ice at 9:55 P.M. It finished at 10:05 P.M. How long did it take to scrape the ice?

___ minutes

Polar Animals

• Antonyms

Polar Opposites

Polar Opposites

soft	hard
fast	slow
day	night
ask	tell
start	stop
take	give
late	early
icy	warm

South Pole	North Pole

The habitats of polar bears and penguins set the stage for this independent activity. Ask each student to fold a sheet of construction paper in half lengthwise and then unfold the paper and flatten it. Also have her cut out a copy of the antonym cards on page 44. A student glues the title card at the top of the construction paper and the penguin and polar bear cards at the bottom, on opposite sides of the fold line. Next, she pairs word cards that have opposite meanings and glues the pairs on her paper as shown. For a finishing touch, ask students to draw colorful lines to connect the words of each antonym pair.

Addition • • • • • • • • • • • • • • • • • **Math**

Icy Calculations

Here's a partner approach to computation practice that is "way cool"! Have each partner write ten different numbers (two, three, or four digits) on a blank sheet of white paper and trim the paper into the shape of an ice floe. To begin, each student circles a number on his ice floe. Then he writes the numbers he and his partner selected on his math paper in the form of an addition problem. He solves the problem and compares his sum to his partner's. If the sums match, the partners repeat the activity with new numbers. If the sums do not match, the partners recheck their calculations until they agree upon a sum. Computation practice is complete when every number has been used.

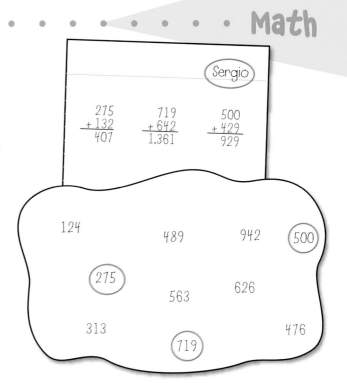

Whether you head north or south for polar explorations, we've got you covered with skill review!

Multiplication facts • • • • • • • • • • • • • • • Math

Sniffing Out Seals

Basic facts are reinforced during this variation of the Battleship partner game. Tell students that polar bears have such an exceptional sense of smell that they can sniff out seal dens buried in layers of snow and ice. Then hand out student copies of the game-board on page 44. Instruct each child to use a crayon to outline five boxes, or seal dens, on the multiplication table. Explain that the object of the game is to find your partner's dens. Pair students and have them name multiplication facts and answers in turn. When a seal den is found, the square is colored. The first player to find all five dens wins the game!

Language Arts • • • • • • • • • • • • Homophones

Penguin Pals

A few penguin observations make this booklet a great spelling reference! Give each child two half sheets of paper (4½" x 12"). Instruct her to stack the papers and then fold them forward to make four graduated layers. Staple her stack near the fold. Remind the class that a penguin's beak can be orange, red, bright purple, or black and its feet can be black, blue, or pink. Then ask each child to illustrate two or more penguins on the front cover, title the cover "Penguin Pals," and label the pages for the homophones *there, their,* and *they're.* To finish each booklet page, she writes a penguin-related sentence that incorporates the featured homophone.

Polar Animals **41**

All That Blubber

Bring the enormous size of some polar animals into view. Post a cutout of a simple balance scale like the one shown. Then make a copy of page 45, cut out the animal pictures, and keep the animal facts for reference. Ask each child to color his self-likeness on each of three paper squares. To begin, display an animal picture in one pan of the scale and announce its weight. Then have students add their drawings to the empty pan until the scale is balanced. (Use an average per student weight such as 60 pounds to calculate the number of drawings needed.) Repeat the activity for each remaining polar animal.

Comprehension · · · · · · · · · · · · · · · ·

Organizing Facts

During this large-group activity students see firsthand how arranging facts on a chart enhances understanding. Allow time for each student to make a set of the animal cards on page 45. To do this, a child cuts along the bold lines on her copy, folds along the thin lines, and then glues together the blank sides of each card. Next, draw and label a simple chart on the board (see illustration). Enlist your students' help in organizing the related information from their cards onto the chart. Ask questions that require students to interpret the organized information and then have each child summarize her learnings in writing.

Animal	Weighs Over 1,000 Pounds	Eats Meat	Eats Plants	Is Part of a Herd	Is a Good Swimmer
Musk Ox			X	X	
Polar Bear	X	X	X		X
Walrus	X	X		X	X

On Location

This small-group activity gets students thinking about polar animals, their physical characteristics, and their habitats. Give each group a large sheet of paper to title "North Pole" or "South Pole." Then challenge the members of each group to list ten or more plural nouns that can be seen at their assigned location. Encourage students to think creatively. Set aside time for each group to display its list and read it aloud. Then have students search the lists to find examples of different plural spellings. Conclude by having each child complete a copy of page 46. To encourage self-checking, tell students that the sum of the numbers they write should total 38.

South Pole
- penguins
- babies
- beaks
- eggs
- bellies
- birds
- flippers
- nests
- rookeries
- moms
- dads

North Pole
- polar bears
- foxes
- ice floes
- claws
- seals
- walruses
- birds
- noses
- cubs
- feathers
- musk oxen

Polar Chitchat

Use the cube pattern on page 47 to get a small or large group of students talking about polar animals. Color the artwork and cut out the pattern. Then fold on the thin lines and use tape to assemble the cube. Start by sitting with students in a circle on the floor. Announce a previously reviewed word, such as *camouflage, habitat, adaptation,* or *migration,* and pass the cube to a student to roll. If the child rolls "This word makes me think of…" or "This word reminds me of…" he completes the sentence and explains why. If he rolls a different side of the cube, he follows the direction. Then he hands the cube to the next student. To continue, announce the same word or a different one. Repeat the activity until every student takes a turn.

Antonym Cards
Use with "Polar Opposites" on page 40.

Polar Opposites

TEC60988

day	soft	take	slow
start	fast	late	tell
ask	hard	night	early
South Pole	North Pole	stop	warm
		icy	give

Gameboard
Use with "Sniffing Out Seals" on page 41.

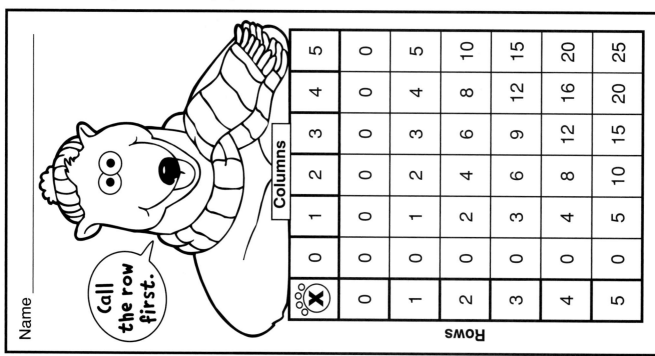

©The Mailbox® • Organize January Now!™ • TEC60988

• **Animal Cards**

Use with "All That Blubber" and "Organizing Facts" on page 42.

Walrus

- can weigh 3,000 pounds
- two long tusks, or teeth
- good swimmer
- part of a herd
- eats only meat
- thick layer of fat
- flippers

TEC60988

Polar Bear

- can weigh 1,400 pounds
- good swimmer
- not part of a herd
- eats plants and meat
- thick layer of fat
- thick coat of fur
- furry paws

TEC60988

Musk Ox

- can weigh 750 pounds
- two curved horns
- part of a herd
- eats only plants
- thick coat of shaggy hair
- longest hair of any mammal
- hooves

TEC60988

Polar Animals 45

Champion Traveler

Use the code.
Circle each plural noun.
Number the box to show
   how the plural was made.

North Pole

Plurals Code

1 = Add **s.**

2 = Add **es.**

3 = Change **y** to **i** and add **es.**

4 = Change spelling.

foxes	fox	
baby	babies	
walrus	walruses	
feet	foot	
bear	bears	
branch	branches	
berries	berry	
whale	whales	
tooth	teeth	
paws	paw	
oxen	ox	
penguin	penguins	
pouches	pouch	
belly	bellies	
dens	den	
goose	geese	

See you at the South Pole!

©The Mailbox® • *Organize January Now!*™ • TEC60988 • Key p. 95

Note to the teacher: Use alone or with "On Location" on page 43.

"Snow" Much Fun!

Creating this CD snowflake will be a blizzard of fun!

Materials for one snowflake:
2 winter pictures (photographs or student-drawn pictures)
2 CDs (free promotional ones that come in the mail)
4 pipe cleaners, each cut into thirds
12" length of yarn
craft glue

Steps:
1. Twist two pipe cleaner pieces together as shown. Repeat with the remaining pieces.
2. Glue the six pipe cleaner twists to the nonshiny side of one CD and allow to dry.
3. Glue the second CD to the first CD (shiny sides out) so that the pipe cleaners are sandwiched between the two CDs.
4. Loop and tie the yarn through the center hole.
5. Glue one picture to each side of the shiny snowflake.

Have a Ball!

Welcome the new year with this dazzling decoration that resembles the famous New Year's Eve Ball at Times Square! First, color and cut out a copy of the patterns on page 50. Next, cut out a six-inch white construction paper circle. Decorate the circle with craft supplies such as rhinestones and glitter. Once the patterns are attached with glue, the ball is ready to display!

Lifting Up the World

To honor Dr. Martin Luther King Jr., make a copy of the globe pattern on page 51 for each child. Have him color and cut out the pattern. After he discusses with his classmates different ways Dr. King helped others, he writes in the space provided three to five sentences that describe how he could help others as well. Next, he traces and colors his hands on unlined paper. Then he cuts out the tracings and glues them to the pattern as shown.

I can help others... by raising money.

Winter Wonderland

To bring the glistening snow indoors, fold a white paper plate in half and then into thirds as shown. Next, cut out different shapes from the edges of the folded plate. Unfold the plate and decorate the resulting snowflake using craft supplies such as glitter and colorful yarn. Display the completed projects to create an indoor winter wonderland.

Countdown Patterns
Use with "Have a Ball!" on page 48.

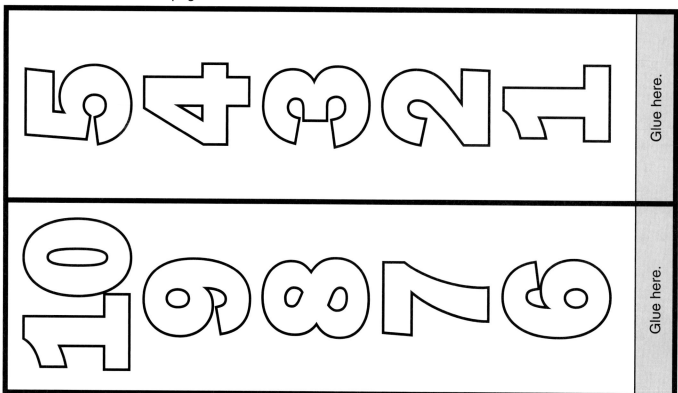

I can help others...

TEC60988

Bulletin Boards &

Copy the bowl and spoon patterns on page 54 onto colorful paper. Cut out the patterns and store them near a board titled as shown. To recommend a book, a child fills in the information on a bowl cutout and posts it on the board. When another student reads that book, he records his name and opinion of the book on a spoon cutout and adds it to the bowl. What an inviting place to find a great book for a cold day!

Hats off to winter! Title a board as shown and give each child an enlarged copy of the hat pattern on page 55. On the brim, have her explain how to do her favorite winter activity. In the space above the brim, have her illustrate the activity. Once she glues a cotton ball to the top of the hat, it's ready to display!

Displays

To warm up a winter day, give each child a 3½" x 12" strip of colorful construction paper to fold in half. Have her trace a copy of the sunglasses pattern on page 54 along the paper's folded edge and cut out the tracing. Once she unfolds the sunglasses cutout, she glues to each lens a magazine picture of a warmer place. After she labels and decorates the sunglasses, she adds them to a display titled as shown.

Decorate a wall with a snowy scene, a happy snowman, and the title shown. Have each child fold an 8½" x 11" sheet of unlined paper into fourths, line up a copy of the snowflake pattern on page 55 with the folded edges, and trace it. She cuts out the tracing and unfolds it. Then she labels it with six of her favorite book titles or authors, makes it sparkle by adding glitter glue, and adds it to the display!

Bowl and Spoon Patterns
Use with "'Souper' Stories" on page 52.

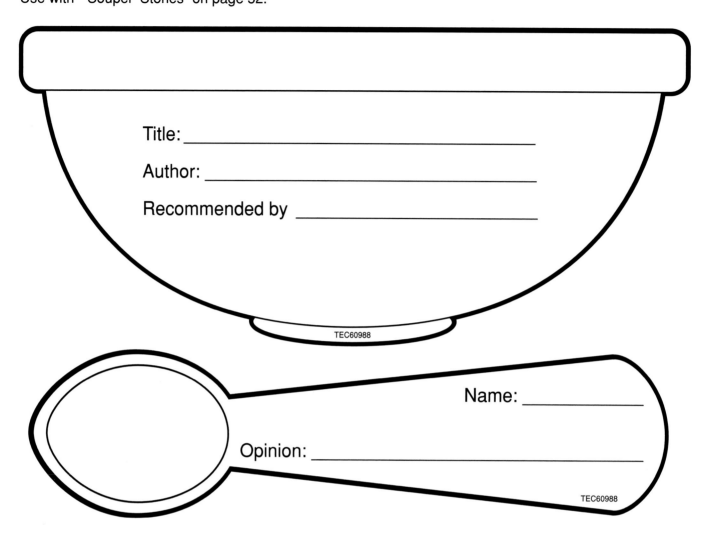

Title: _____

Author: _____

Recommended by _____

TEC60988

Name: _____

Opinion: _____

TEC60988

Sunglasses Pattern
Use with "Dreaming of Warmer Places!" on page 53.

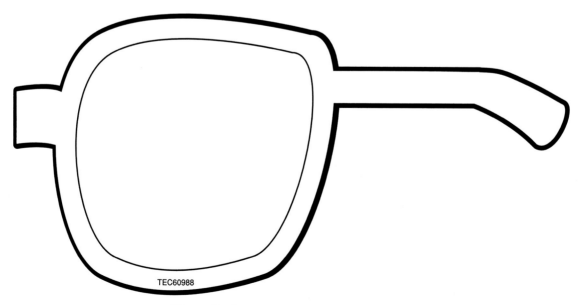

TEC60988

©The Mailbox® • *Organize January Now!*™ • TEC60988

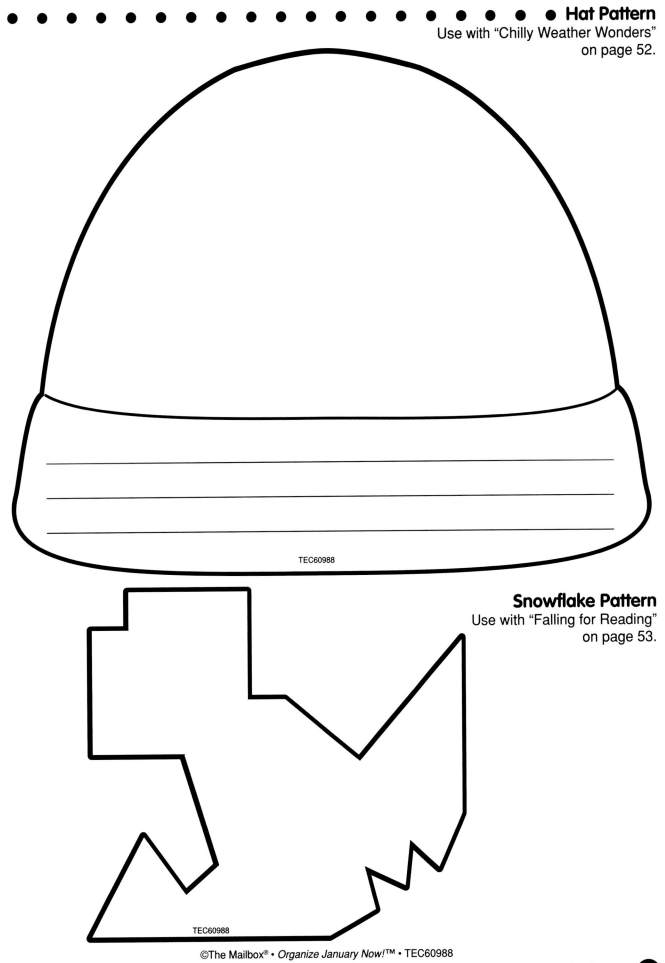

TEC60988

Snowflake Pattern
Use with "Falling for Reading"
on page 53.

TEC60988

Centers

Math

Faces, edges, and corners

Mystery Shapes

Label pieces of masking tape as shown, and tape them to a pair of adult-size fuzzy mittens. Put a different solid figure in each mitten. Place the mittens at a center along with several copies of the recording sheet from page 58. To use the center, a child puts his hand in mitten 1, feels the shape inside it without looking, and guesses the shape. Then he removes the object from the mitten and completes the recording sheet. He repeats the process again with the second mitten.

Mitten 1

Mitten 2

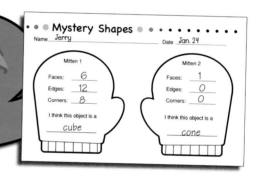

• • ● **Mystery Shapes** ● • • • • • •
Name ___Jerry___   Date ___Jan. 24___

Mitten 1
Faces: ___6___
Edges: ___12___
Corners: ___8___
I think this object is a
___cube___

Mitten 2
Faces: ___1___
Edges: ___0___
Corners: ___0___
I think this object is a
___cone___

Plurals ending in -ies

Language Arts

Ice Fishing

Program several colorful copies of the fish patterns on page 58 with singular nouns whose plural forms end in *-ies.* Attach a metal paper clip to each fish and place all the fish in a bucket or shoebox. To make a fishing pole, tie a length of string to one end of a wooden rod and attach a small magnet to the string's loose end as shown. Then place the materials at a center along with paper. To use the center, a child fishes for a noun. When she catches one, she pulls it in and writes its plural form on a piece of paper. Once she catches all of the fish, she uses a dictionary to check each answer.

bunny

party

Probability, fractions

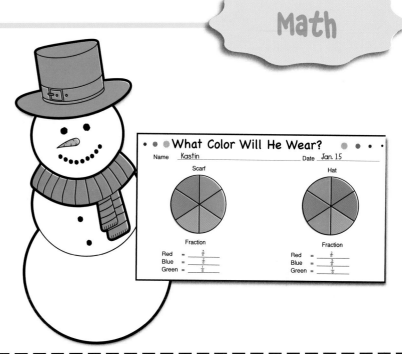

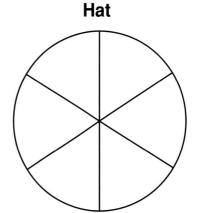

Dress the Snowman!

Make one copy of the snowman pattern on page 59. Also make five red copies, three blue copies, and two green copies of the hat and scarf patterns on page 59. Put the scarf and hat cutouts in separate paper bags and place them at a center along with the copy of the snowman, several copies of the recording sheet below, and red, green, and blue crayons. To use the center, a child draws one accessory from each bag, places it on the snowman, and then colors a section of each pie chart the matching color. She returns the items to the bag and draws again, continuing in this manner until both charts are completely colored. Then she writes a fraction for each chart to represent each color.

What Color Will He Wear?

Name_____   Date _____

Scarf

Hat

Fraction

Fraction

Red   = _____
Blue   = _____
Green = _____

Red   = _____
Blue   = _____
Green = _____

©The Mailbox® • *Organize January Now!*™ • TEC60988

Mystery Shapes

Name_____ Date _____

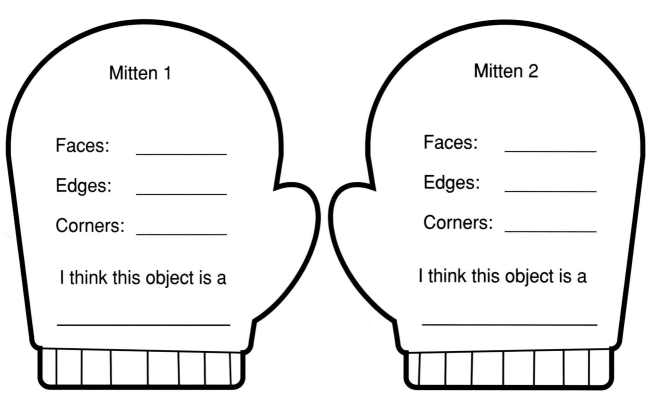

Mitten 1

Faces: _____

Edges: _____

Corners: _____

I think this object is a

_____

Mitten 2

Faces: _____

Edges: _____

Corners: _____

I think this object is a

_____

©The Mailbox® • *Organize January Now!*™ • TEC60988

Note to the teacher: Use with "Mystery Shapes" on page 56.

Fish Patterns ●
Use with "Ice Fishing" on page 56 and "Stump the Penguins!" on page 60.

TEC60988

TEC60988

©The Mailbox® • *Organize January Now!*™ • TEC60988

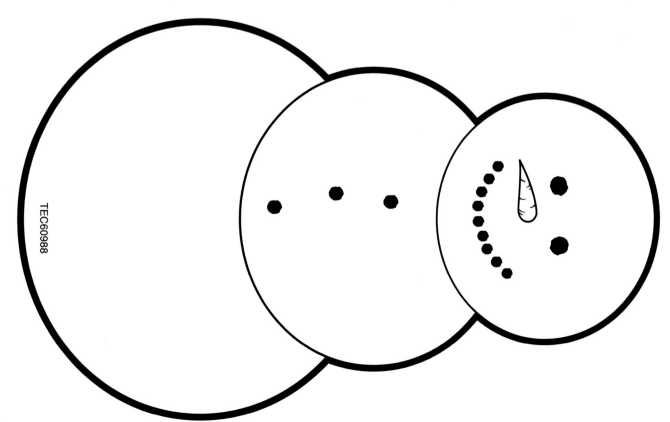

TEC60988

Games

Language Arts

Spelling

Stump the Penguins!

For this whole-class game, prepare a supply of fish cutouts (patterns on page 58). Then divide students into small teams. Have the members of Team 1 stand at the front of the room and represent penguins on an iceberg. Explain that each seated team, in turn, will try to stump the penguins by challenging them to spell a word from a teacher-provided list of words. The penguins must work together to spell the word. If they spell it correctly, they are awarded one fish cutout. If they spell the word incorrectly, then the team that selected the word gets the fish. After all of the teams have had a turn at stumping the penguins, members of Team 2 become the penguins. Play continues in this manner until the members of every team have been penguins. The team with the most cutouts at the end of the game wins.

Vocabulary

Science & Social Studies

Snowball Toss

In advance, write each vocabulary word for a new science or social studies unit on a separate snowball-shaped cutout. Place the cutouts on a table. Invite student pairs to choose a snowball to pass back and forth. Explain that before a partner passes the snowball, he must either define or state a fact about the word on the snowball. The last partner able to say something about the word wins that round. Then the partners select a new snowball to toss.

Probability

Button Up!

Give each pair of students two copies of page 62 and a pair of dice. Each player cuts apart the button cards at the bottom of her gameboard. She thinks about the sums that could be rolled with the dice and then strategically places any number of her 12 buttons on any of those snowmen. Player 1 rolls the dice. If she has a button on the snowman that's labeled with the sum rolled, she removes one button from that snowman. If she does not have a button on that snowman, she does nothing. Partners continue taking turns in this manner until one player removes all of the buttons from her snowmen and wins.

Language Arts

Possessive pronouns

A Blizzard of Pronouns

Give each pair of players a copy of page 63, scissors, a brown paper lunch sack, and two different-colored crayons. The pair cuts apart the sentence strips and puts them in the sack. Next, each player chooses a crayon. To begin the game, Player 1 pulls a strip from the bag and reads the sentence aloud, filling in the blank with the correct possessive pronoun that completes the sentence. She checks the answer key (page 95). If her answer is correct, she colors a snowflake containing the matching pronoun. If she is incorrect, she returns the strip to the bag and then her turn is over. If there is no snowflake with that pronoun left to color, she colors nothing. Then Player 2 takes a turn in the same manner. Partners continue taking turns until there are no more strips in the sack. Then they record scores to determine a winner.

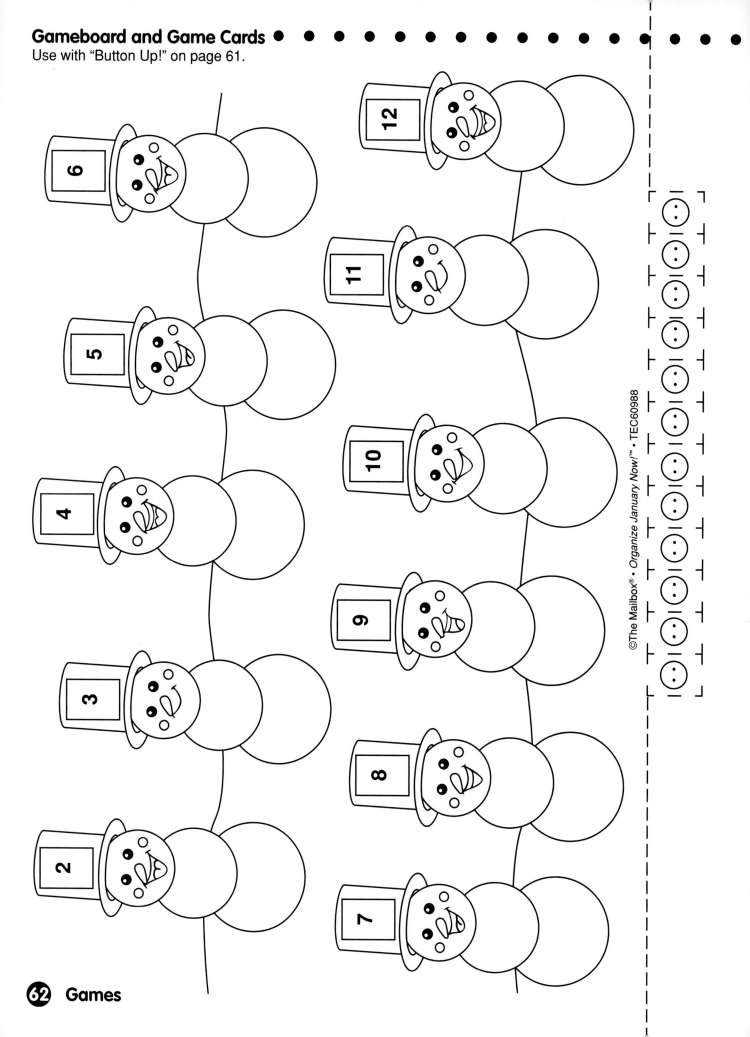

©The Mailbox® • *Organize January Now!*™ • TEC60988

Name _____ Score _____
Name _____ Score _____

her your her his my her
his his her her my his your
my his my my your my
her

©The Mailbox® • *Organize January Now!*™ • TEC60988

1. The blue mittens belong to me.
   They are ___ mittens.

2. Sue will shovel the sidewalk.
   It is ___ turn.

3. Did you buy these boots?
   Are these ___ boots?

4. The boy carried a toy to the door.
   He wants to take ___ toy outside.

5. Chuck has a red scarf.
   Red is ___ favorite color.

6. Did you bring this sled?
   Is it ___ sled?

7. Does this water bottle belong to Dan?
   Is it ___ water bottle?

8. I brought these ice skates.
   They are ___ best skates!

9. Those are Mom's boots.
   They are ___ boots.

10. I will drink hot cocoa.
    It is ___ favorite treat.

11. Bill owns the blue sled.
    It is ___ sled.

12. Did Denise drink some cocoa?
    Is this ___ mug?

13. The pink earmuffs are Mary's.
    They are ___ earmuffs.

14. I have a brown puppy.
    It is ___ dog.

15. Carl has black boots.
    They are ___ boots.

16. Do you want to sled now?
    It is ___ turn.

17. I am wearing an orange scarf.
    It is ___ scarf.

18. She bought a new hat.
    It is ___ hat.

Management Tips

A Blizzard of Great Work

Turn unused wall space into a wintry display of your students' best efforts! Hot-glue a clothespin to a poster board snowflake for each child. Mount the cutouts on the wall within students' reach. Invite each child to clip a sample of his work to one of the clothespins. Have him replace the sample whenever he has a new one he's eager to display.

Marshmallow Motivator

For an incentive that encourages students to turn in homework on time, make a colorful copy of the mug pattern on page 65 for each child. Program the mug with the child's name and then display the mugs where students can easily reach them. Then make a supply of the marshmallow patterns on page 65. Each time a child turns in her homework on time, allow her to add a marshmallow to her mug. When students have a predetermined number of marshmallows in their mugs, treat them to a hot cocoa party!

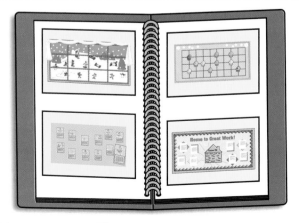

Easy Recall

Looking for an easy way to keep track of seasonal bulletin boards? Try this! Take a photo of each classroom bulletin board and wall or door display and then arrange the pictures chronologically in an album. Next year, you'll have the ideas at your fingertips!

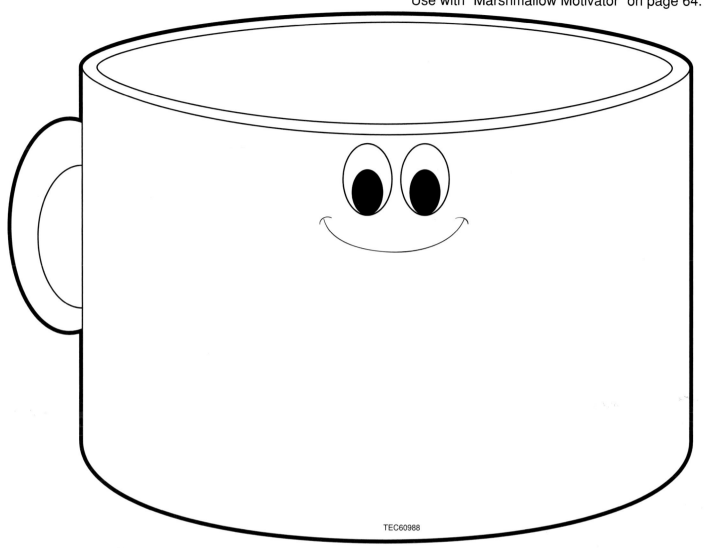

TEC60988

"I'm so glad you made me! I love being seen by all the kids!" the snowman said.

"Oh, no! The sun is coming out! I don't want to melt away!" the snowman cried.

In Someone Else's Shoes

The next time a student has a few minutes to fill, ask him to pretend he's a snowman or another wintry being. Then have him write sentences with correct punctuation that include phrases or expressions he might say as that character on a cold, wintry day. He'll not only have practiced writing from a different perspective, but he will have practiced grammar skills to boot!

Puzzled Pictures

For this spatial awareness activity, mount a picture from an old winter calendar onto a colorful sheet of construction paper. Use a paper cutter to cut the picture into several angled pieces; then put the pieces in a resealable bag. After a student finishes her work, allow her to put the puzzle together at her desk. If desired, create several calendar puzzles in this way, using a different color of paper for each one to make it easier to return a stray piece to the correct bag.

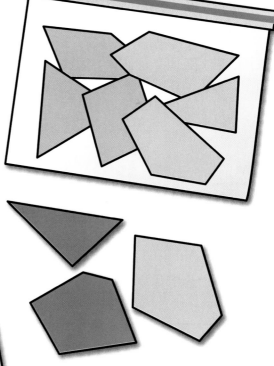

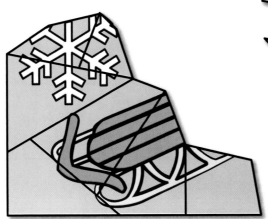

Word Storm

Reinforce subject-verb agreement with this easy time filler. Write on the board a seasonal noun such as *polar bear.* Have students try to write as many action verbs as there are letters in the word(s), making sure that the noun and verb agree in number. If desired, invite each child to use some of her words to write a fun seasonal poem.

polar bear

hunts
fishes
roars
sleeps

3, 2, 1 Countdown

When it comes to number sense, this patterning activity is first-rate! Provide each child with a copy of a hundred chart. Instruct him to find and color a number pattern that counts down the hours it could take for a snowman to melt. After the student colors the chart, have him write three clues that describe his pattern. Then invite him to read his clues aloud and have his classmates try to guess the pattern.

1	2	3	4	5	6	7	8	9	10
11	12	13	14	15	16	17	18	19	20
21	22	23	24	25	26	27	28	29	30
31	32	33	34	35	36	37	38	39	40
41	42	43	44	45	46	47	48	49	50
51	52	53	54	55	56	57	58	59	60
61	62	63	64	65	66	67	68	69	70
71	72	73	74	75	76	77	78	79	80
81	82	83	84	85	86	87	88	89	90
91	92	93	94	95	96	97	98	99	100

There are even and odd numbers in my countdown.

All of the numbers in my countdown are in two columns on the hundred chart.

All of the numbers in my countdown end in either 0 or 5.

100, 95, 90, 85...all melted!

Journal Prompts

- Pretend you are a penguin that is afraid of the water. How will you solve this problem? Write about it.

- Describe three things that you hope you can do this year.

- Which of these winter sports do you like the best: basketball, snow skiing, or ice hockey? Explain.

- Imagine a snowstorm with purple snow. How would it be the same as a regular snowstorm? How would it be different?

- Make a list of words that begin with w. Circle all of the words that could be used to describe winter.

- Some things are best when they are brand-new. Some things are best when you have had them for a while. Describe your favorite new and old things.

Choose one of these ready-to-go writing ideas to use with the penguin pattern on page 70.

- Program a copy of the pattern with a journal prompt from above; then make a class supply.

- On a copy of the pattern, have each youngster write about the coolest thing she has ever done. Then have students post their finished work atop white construction paper ice mounds on a bulletin board titled "Cool Writing."

- Share with students the penguin facts shown. Then give each child a copy of the pattern to use to compare and contrast how he stays warm in the winter with how a penguin does.

Penguins seem very different than me, but we both have to stay warm. Some penguins have extra layers of feathers that keep them warm. I wear layers of clothes to stay warm. My layers are clothes, not feathers. Feathers keep penguins from getting wet. I wear a coat to keep warm and dry when it snows.

_____ Joshua

Penguin Facts
- Penguins spend most of their time in the ocean.
- Penguin feathers are short and thick.
- A penguin's feathers help make a waterproof coat.
- A penguin has layers of blubber that help it stay warm.
- Some penguins have extra layers of soft feathers that keep them warm.

Prompts

Warming Up for Winter
Descriptive Writing

For a seasonal writing activity that's perfect for partners, collect winter accessories such as socks, caps, scarves, gloves, or mittens. Give each student pair one wintry accessory to describe from the item's point of view (without naming the item). When all students have finished writing, collect the descriptions and have the partners sit side by side in a circle with their accessories before them. Then read aloud each pair's description, challenging students to point out the matching accessory.

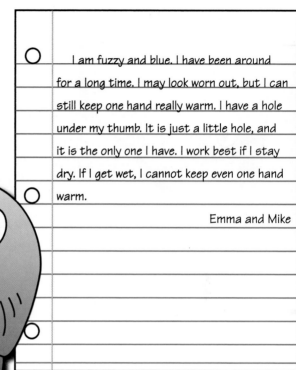

I am fuzzy and blue. I have been around for a long time. I may look worn out, but I can still keep one hand really warm. I have a hole under my thumb. It is just a little hole, and it is the only one I have. I work best if I stay dry. If I get wet, I cannot keep even one hand warm.

Emma and Mike

Nippy Notes
Persuasive Writing

Have students write letters to convince Old Man Winter to make winter one month longer or one month shorter. To begin, have each student think about whether he likes or dislikes winter. Guide him to brainstorm two details that support his view and then draft his letter. Have the youngster write his final draft on a copy of page 71. Assemble the pages in a class book titled "Dear Old Man Winter."

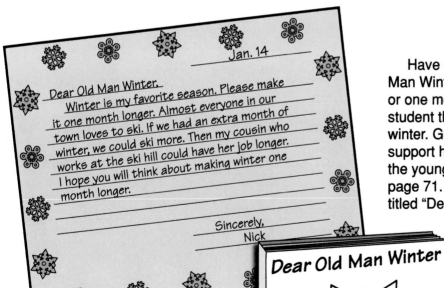

Jan. 14

Dear Old Man Winter,
    Winter is my favorite season. Please make it one month longer. Almost everyone in our town loves to ski. If we had an extra month of winter, we could ski more. Then my cousin who works at the ski hill could have her job longer. I hope you will think about making winter one month longer.

Sincerely,
Nick

Dear Old Man Winter

Penguin Pattern ● ● ● ● ● ● ● ● ● ● ● ● ● ● ●
Use with the writing prompts and
ideas on page 68.

©The Mailbox® • *Organize January Now!*™ • TEC60988

TEC60988

Frosty Friends

A ready-to-use center mat and cards for two different learning levels

Two-digit subtraction without regrouping
Two-digit subtraction with regrouping

Materials:
center mat to the right
number cards and answer key cards on page 75
copies of the recording sheet on page 77
2 resealable plastic bags

Preparing the center:
Cut out each set of color-coded cards. Store each set of cards (including the answer key) in a bag. Select the card set that makes the best skill review for your students. Store the remaining card set for later use.

Using the center:
1. A student places the heart card and the answer key on the mat as directed.
2. She lays a button card in the yellow box.
3. She writes and solves the problem in a blank box on her recording sheet.
4. She checks the answer key. If her answer is there, she colors the button in the box. If her answer is not there, she reworks the problem until it is.
5. She moves the button card to a discard pile.
6. She repeats Steps 2 through 5 for each remaining button card.

Frosty Friends

Snowflake Inn

Put heart card here.

Put answer key here.

To make a problem, lay a button card in the yellow box.

Write and solve the problem on page 77.

Use with the directions on page 72.

(no regrouping required)	978	– 263	– 745
– 574	– 626	– 177	– 852
– 318	– 454	– 431	– 643

Answer Key

126
233
335
352
404
524
547
660
715
801

(regrouping required)	562	– 414	– 136
– 333	– 225	– 390	– 447
– 181	– 103	– 358	– 272

Answer Key

115
148
172
204
229
290
337
381
426
459

Frosty Friends
TEC60988

Frosty Friends
TEC60988

Frosty Friends
TEC60988

Frosty Friends
TEC60988

Frosty Friends
TEC60988

Frosty Friends
TEC60988

Frosty Friends
TEC60988

Frosty Friends
TEC60988

Frosty Friends
TEC60988

Frosty Friends
TEC60988

Frosty Friends
TEC60988

Frosty Friends
TEC60988

Frosty Friends
TEC60988

Frosty Friends
TEC60988

Frosty Friends
TEC60988

Frosty Friends
TEC60988

Frosty Friends
TEC60988

Frosty Friends
TEC60988

Frosty Friends
TEC60988

Frosty Friends
TEC60988

Frosty Friends
TEC60988

Frosty Friends
TEC60988

Frosty Friends
TEC60988

Frosty Friends

Name _____ Date _____

Write and solve a subtraction problem in each box.
If your answer is on the center mat, color the button.
If it is not, rework the problem.

Cuckoo Cub

A ready-to-use center mat and cards

Materials:
center mat to the right
supporting detail cards on page 81
copies of the recording sheet on page 83
resealable plastic bag

Preparing the center:
Cut out the cards and store them in the plastic bag.

Using the center:
1. A student stacks the cards faceup.
2. She reads the detail on the top card.
3. She decides which main idea it supports and places the card in the matching box.
4. She continues in this manner until all the cards are sorted.
5. She completes a copy of the recording sheet.

Cuckoo Cub

Match each card to a main idea.
Complete page 83.

Mom, look at me!

A baby polar bear is called a cub.

A polar bear's habitat is very cold.

A polar bear is a strong swimmer.

Use with the directions on page 78.

has big front paws with webbed toes
swims long distances
swims underwater
holds its breath for a long time
has a thick and waterproof coat
is born inside a den of snow
weighs less than two pounds at birth
grows very quickly
stays with its mom for up to three years
is curious and playful
is near the North Pole
has lots of ice and snow
is close to shorelines and sea ice
is dark during the winter
has very cold winds

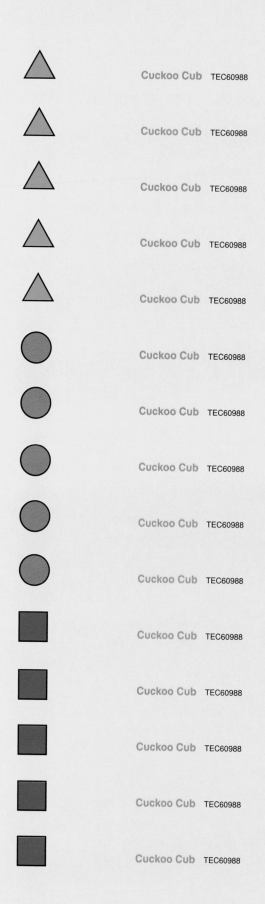

Cuckoo Cub TEC60988

Cuckoo Cub TEC60988

Cuckoo Cub TEC60988

Cuckoo Cub TEC60988

Cuckoo Cub TEC60988

Cuckoo Cub TEC60988

Cuckoo Cub TEC60988

Cuckoo Cub TEC60988

Cuckoo Cub TEC60988

Cuckoo Cub TEC60988

Cuckoo Cub TEC60988

Cuckoo Cub TEC60988

Cuckoo Cub TEC60988

Cuckoo Cub TEC60988

Cuckoo Cub TEC60988

A Curious Cub

Name_____ Date _____

Flip over each set of cards to check your work.
Copy the main idea for each symbol.

△ _____

○ _____

□ _____

Read each detail below.
If it supports a main idea from above, draw the matching symbol.
If it does not, draw an X.

1. _____ winter temperatures can drop to –50°F.

2. _____ swims underwater

3. _____ cannot hear or see when it is born

4. _____ learns to hunt from its mother

5. _____ roams the ice alone in search of food

6. _____ drinks milk from its mother

7. _____ paddles with its large front paws

8. _____ trees cannot grow there

Note to the teacher: Use with the directions on page 78.

Signs of Snow

Name _____

Date _____

Add *mis-* or *pre-* to each word.
Write each new word on the correct sign.

fit

soak

heat

pay

count

use

cook

deed

school

lead

place

view

spell

game

mis-	pre-
_____	_____
_____	_____
_____	_____
_____	_____
_____	_____
_____	_____
_____	_____

Lost Mittens

Match each definition to a word on the basket. Color by the code.

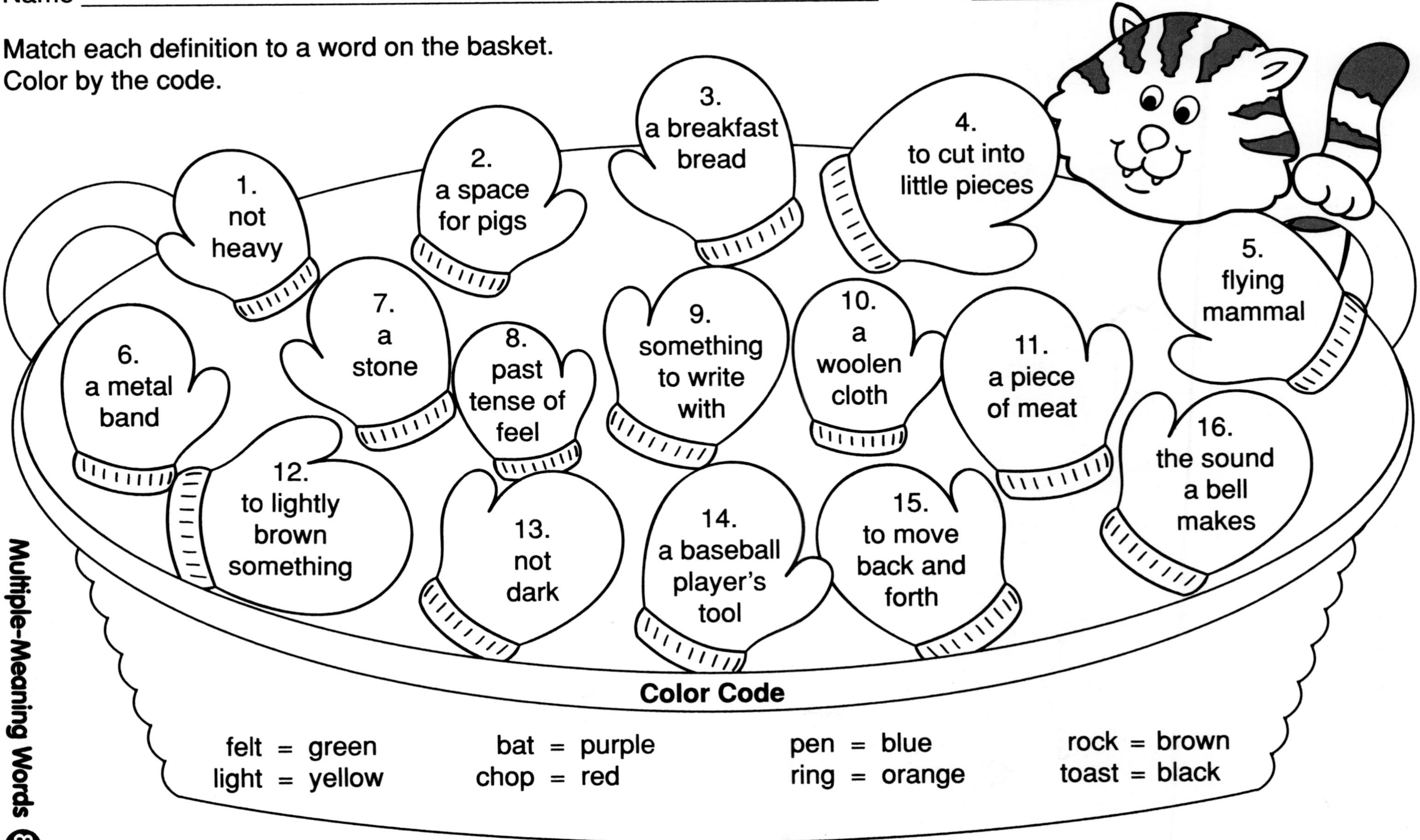

1. not heavy

2. a space for pigs

3. a breakfast bread

4. to cut into little pieces

5. flying mammal

6. a metal band

7. a stone

8. past tense of feel

9. something to write with

10. a woolen cloth

11. a piece of meat

12. to lightly brown something

13. not dark

14. a baseball player's tool

15. to move back and forth

16. the sound a bell makes

Color Code

felt = green	rock = brown
light = yellow	toast = black
bat = purple	pen = blue
chop = red	ring = orange

©The Mailbox® • *Organize January Now!*™ • TEC60988 • Key p. 96

Multiple-Meaning Words 85

Snow Day

Name _____ Date _____

Write the coordinates for each object.

A. snow skis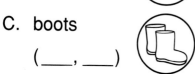
   (___, ___)

B. ski poles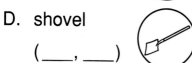
   (___, ___)

C. boots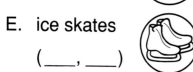
   (___, ___)

D. shovel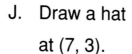
   (___, ___)

E. ice skates
   (___, ___)

Follow the directions.

F. Draw a hockey stick at (5, 3).

G. Draw a hockey puck at (1, 5).

H. Draw a mitten at (2, 2).

I. Draw a glove at (4, 1).

J. Draw a hat at (7, 3).

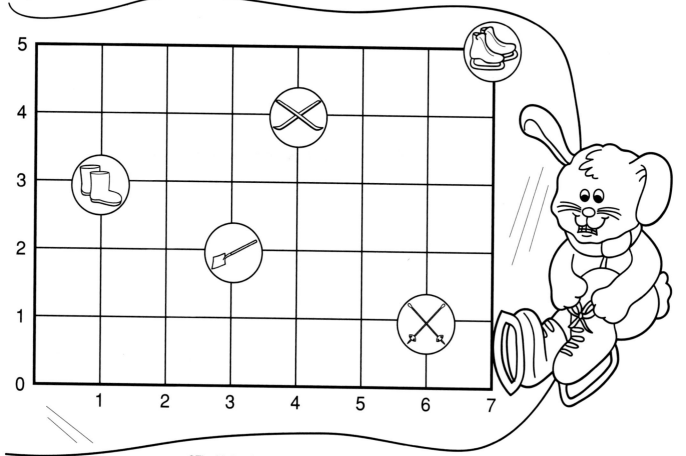

Hockey Friends

Name_____ Date _____

Look at the punctuation in each sentence.
Color the hockey puck in the matching column.

	Correct	Incorrect
1. "This is a great game! Ron said.	B	O
2. "Thanks for the ticket," said Chuck.	B	S
3. Mike said, "The Fleas are my favorite team!"	R	H
4. Did you see that play? Chuck asked.	L	M
5. "No, I was eating my popcorn, Max said."	S	E
6. Ron said, "I missed it too."	W	M
7. "That player sped across the ice! Chuck yelled."	T	L
8. "Now he's going for a goal!" Ron shouted.	I	M
9. Wow! What a great play! Max said.	R	N
10. "Go team!" the three cheered together.	G	H

What do hockey players hate most about the penalty box?
To solve the riddle, write the letters above in the matching
numbered blanks below.

There's no ___ ___ ___ ___ ___ ___ ___ ___   ___ ___ ___ ___!
       5 7 2 1 6 8 9 10   3 1 1 4

Sonny's Agenda

Name _____

Date _____

Read Sonny's notes about his morning.

8:30 — Feed the birds.
9:30 — Watch the children as they sled.
10:30 — Drink cocoa with snowpals.
11:30 — Read a library book.

Word Bank

first   then
next   last

Write about Sonny's morning.
Use words from the word bank to help you.
Add details and use descriptive words in your writing.

Narrative Writing, Sequencing Events

Sweet Dreams

Name _____   Date _____

Cut apart the digital time cards below.
Glue each card next to the clock that shows the same time.

Wake up.

Drink cocoa.

Swim.

Eat breakfast.

Go fishing.

Eat lunch.

See a movie.

Go sledding.

Eat dinner.

Ice-skate.

11:35	3:40	5:55	9:10	10:35
2:05	7:20	6:50	1:00	8:15

Telling Time to Five Minutes 89

Take a Dive!

Name _____ Date _____

Divide.
Help the penguins find the fish.
Color each bubble with an answer greater than 5.

Start

$6\overline{)12}$ $7\overline{)21}$ $5\overline{)15}$ $1\overline{)8}$ $3\overline{)21}$ $9\overline{)81}$

$4\overline{)32}$ $6\overline{)54}$ $2\overline{)16}$ $8\overline{)64}$ $5\overline{)10}$ $4\overline{)20}$

$7\overline{)49}$ $2\overline{)4}$ $6\overline{)24}$ $4\overline{)12}$ $3\overline{)9}$ $8\overline{)32}$

$6\overline{)42}$ $5\overline{)35}$ $9\overline{)63}$ $4\overline{)8}$ $1\overline{)3}$ $6\overline{)18}$

$3\overline{)27}$ $1\overline{)2}$ $9\overline{)18}$ $4\overline{)4}$

Finish

Division Facts   **Note to the teacher:** Each child will need a crayon to complete this page.

Capitalization

Very Cool!

Write six different reasons to use capital letters.

If you get stuck, study the word bank for clues.

Word Bank

January	Frosty Avenue	Dr. Sniffles
Fluffy	Snow Hill, NC	Mystery at Frozen Pool
Saturday	I	New Year's Day

©The Mailbox® • *Organize January Now!*™ • TEC60988

Vocabulary

What a Pair!

A pair is two like items.
A pair is also one item that has two like parts.

List ten or more pairs.

©The Mailbox® • *Organize January Now!*™ • TEC60988

Write a plan

Happy New Year

Write a wish for the new year. Circle it in blue.

Now write five things you can do to help make your wish come true.

©The Mailbox® • *Organize January Now!*™ • TEC60988

Support an opinion

Symbol of Peace

Draw the animal you think is the best symbol for peace.

Write two or more reasons.

©The Mailbox® • *Organize January Now!*™ • TEC60988

Math Activity Cards

Cut out the cards. Use them as center or free-time activities.

On a Roll
Expanded form

Write four three-digit numbers in standard form.

Then write each number in expanded form. Draw snowballs instead of zeros!

123

1⬡⬡ + 2⬡ + 3

©The Mailbox® • *Organize January Now!*™ • TEC60988

Parts of a Scarf
Fractions

Draw a scarf and divide it into six equal parts. Color the scarf parts. Use fractions to describe your scarf.

My scarf is $\frac{1}{4}$ red, $\frac{1}{4}$ blue, and $\frac{2}{4}$ yellow.

©The Mailbox® • *Organize January Now!*™ • TEC60988

Fashion Forecast
Temperature

Make your paper look like the one shown.

Describe proper clothing for each outdoor temperature.

Fashion Forecast		
30°F	95°F	60°F

—100 F°
—90
—80
—70
—60
—50
—40
—30
—20
—10
—0
—-10
—-20

©The Mailbox® • *Organize January Now!*™ • TEC60988

Tummy Ticklers
Multiplication facts

Use the factors on the penguin.

Write and solve ten or more multiplication facts.

Hee! Hee! Hee!

2 3
0 1
4 5

©The Mailbox® • *Organize January Now!*™ • TEC60988

Answer Keys

Page 22
1. E
2. C
3. B
4. H
5. D
6. A
7. F
8. G

Page 23
1. Un(tie)
2. (loud)est
3. (cold)est
4. Un(lock)
5. (large)r
6. Un(fold)
7. mis(place)
8. (long)er
9. (soon)er
10. mis(behave)

Page 29
1. Martin Luther King Jr. Day is the third Monday in January.
2. Martin Luther King Jr. wanted to see all people treated fairly and equally.
3. Answers may vary. Possible answers include the following: He led marches. He gave speeches. He sometimes sat in silence.
4. Answers will vary but may include the following: brave, leader, speaker.
5. Answers will vary.

Page 30
A. 9
B. 16
C. 14
D. 14
E. 21
F. 20
G. 8
H. 15
I. 14
J. 12

Page 31
A. Sara: hot dogs
   Mark: drinks
   Tyrone: cookies
   Kate: chips
B. Mark, Kate, Sara, Tyrone

Page 38
1. E
2. M
3. P
4. T
5. K
6. I
7. U
8. H
9. A
10. C

Because THE ICE MIGHT CRACK UP!

Page 39
A. 1, 25
B. 35
C. 15
D. 20
E. 40
F. 1, 15
G. 2, 5
H. 10

Page 46

(foxes)	fox	2
baby	(babies)	3
walrus	(walruses)	2
(feet)	foot	4
bear	(bears)	1
branch	(branches)	2
(berries)	berry	3
whale	(whales)	1
tooth	(teeth)	4
(paws)	paw	1
(oxen)	ox	4
penguin	(penguins)	1
(pouches)	pouch	2
belly	(bellies)	3
(dens)	den	1
goose	(geese)	4

Page 61
1. my
2. her
3. your
4. his
5. his
6. your
7. his
8. my
9. her
10. my
11. his
12. her
13. her
14. my
15. his
16. your
17. my
18. her

Page 83

△ A polar bear is a strong swimmer.

◯ A baby polar bear is called a cub.

▢ A polar bear's habitat is very cold.

1. ▢
2. △
3. ◯
4. ◯
5. X
6. ◯
7. △
8. ▢

Page 84

Order may vary.

mis-	pre-
miscount	precook
misfit	pregame
mislead	preview
misplace	preheat
misdeed	presoak
misspell	prepay
misuse	preschool

Page 85

1. light (yellow)
2. pen (blue)
3. toast (black)
4. chop (red)
5. bat (purple)
6. ring (orange)
7. rock (brown)
8. felt (green)
9. pen (blue)
10. felt (green)
11. chop (red)
12. toast (black)
13. light (yellow)
14. bat (purple)
15. rock (brown)
16. ring (orange)

Page 86

A. (4, 4)
B. (6, 1)
C. (1, 3)
D. (3, 2)
E. (7, 5)

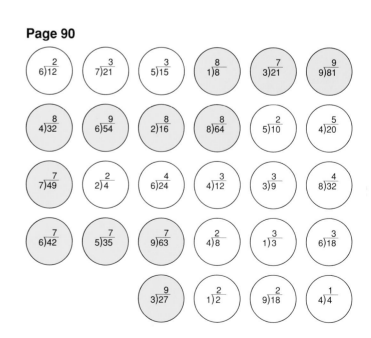

Page 87

1. O
2. B
3. R
4. M
5. E
6. W
7. L
8. I
9. N
10. G

There's no <u>ELBOWING ROOM</u>!

Page 89

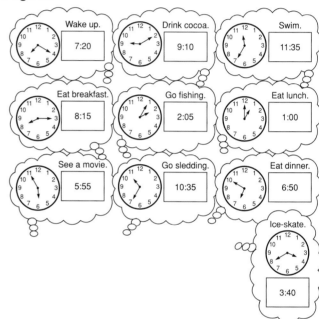

Page 90

(A grid of division problems in circles, some shaded gray:)

$6)\overline{12}$	$7)\overline{21}$	$5)\overline{15}$	$1)\overline{8}$	$3)\overline{21}$	$9)\overline{81}$
$4)\overline{32}$	$6)\overline{54}$	$2)\overline{16}$	$8)\overline{64}$	$5)\overline{10}$	$4)\overline{20}$
$7)\overline{49}$	$2)\overline{4}$	$6)\overline{24}$	$4)\overline{12}$	$3)\overline{9}$	$8)\overline{32}$
$6)\overline{42}$	$5)\overline{35}$	$9)\overline{63}$	$4)\overline{8}$	$1)\overline{3}$	$6)\overline{18}$
$3)\overline{27}$	$1)\overline{2}$	$9)\overline{18}$	$4)\overline{4}$		